SOUTH AFRICA

Written by
Rebecca Phillips-Bartlett

 Gareth Stevens
PUBLISHING

TRAVEL THE WORLD!

Please visit our website, www.garethstevens.com. For a free color catalog of all our high-quality books, call toll free 1-800-542-2595 or fax 1-877-542-2596.

Cataloging-in-Publication Data

Names: Phillips-Bartlett, Rebecca.
Title: South Africa / Rebecca Phillips-Bartlett.
Description: New York : Gareth Stevens Publishing, 2024. | Series: Travel the world!
Identifiers: ISBN 9781538288429 (pbk.) | ISBN 9781538288436 (library bound) | ISBN 9781538288443 (ebook)
Subjects: LCSH: South Africa--Juvenile literature. | South Africa--Description and travel--Juvenile literature.
Classification: LCC DT1719.P455 2024 | DDC 968--dc23

Published in 2024 by
Gareth Stevens Publishing
2544 Clinton St.
Buffalo, NY 14224

Written by: Rebecca Phillips-Bartlett
Edited by: Elise Carraway
Designed by: Amy Li

Photo Credits
All images are courtesy of Shutterstock.com, unless otherwise specified. With thanks to Getty Images, Thinkstock Photo and iStockphoto.
Recurring images – ONYXprj, Ihor Biliavskyi, Olleg, Vector_Up. Cover – Sentavio, LineTale, Sky and glass, PCH.Vector, GoodStudio, IgorMass. 2–3 – Thomas Retterath. 4–5 – AlyonaZhitnaya, chrupka, LeoEdition, GoodStudio, Studio_G. 6–7 – ActiveLines, Boris_V, JONATHAN PLEDGER, klyaksun, Ragulina, WitR, alexmstudio. 8–9 – alexmstudio, fivepointsix, Kelly27, lulu and isabelle, Mike Peel. 10–11 – Alexius1968, klyaksun, Neissl, ProStockStudio, Rich T Photo, Sky and glass, U. Eisenlohr. 12–13 – ActiveLines, Brian van Niekerk SA, Davies Peace Design, EcoPrint, Jennifer Sophie, Modvector, Wildeside. 14–15 – Amanita Silvicora, Benny Marty, Charmaine A Harvey, Janettavr, klyaksun, MD_Photography. 16–17 – Amanita Silvicora, Carcharadon, Colorapt Media, Hajakely, klyaksun, Natursports, Sensvector. 18–19 – Grobler du Preez, LineTale, Olaf Holland, Vanessa Bentley. 20–21 – Denis Mironov, John Martin Media, LineTale, NMacTavish, Roger de la Harpe, Sergey Uryadnikov. 22–23 – GoodStudio, Irina Solatges, addinia.

© 2023 Booklife Publishing
This edition is published by arrangement with Booklife Publishing

All rights reserved. No part of this book may be reproduced in any form without permission in writing from the publisher, except by a reviewer.

Printed in the United States of America

CPSIA compliance information: Batch #CSGS24: For further information contact Gareth Stevens at 1-800-542-2595.

Find us on

CONTENTS

PAGE 4	We Are Going on a Trip	PAGE 15	Bathurst
PAGE 6	Kruger National Park	PAGE 16	Addo Elephant National Park
PAGE 7	Motlatse Canyon	PAGE 17	Cape Agulhas
PAGE 8	Cradle of Humankind	PAGE 18	Afrikaans Language Monument
PAGE 9	Sterkfontein Caves	PAGE 19	Cape Town: V and A Waterfront
PAGE 10	Johannesburg	PAGE 20	Table Mountain
PAGE 11	iSimangaliso Wetland Park	PAGE 21	False Bay
PAGE 12	Drakensberg	PAGE 22	Home
PAGE 13	The Big Hole	PAGE 24	Glossary and Index
PAGE 14	Tsitsikamma Forest and the Big Tree		

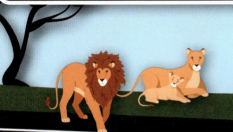

WORDS THAT LOOK LIKE THIS CAN BE FOUND IN THE GLOSSARY ON PAGE 24.

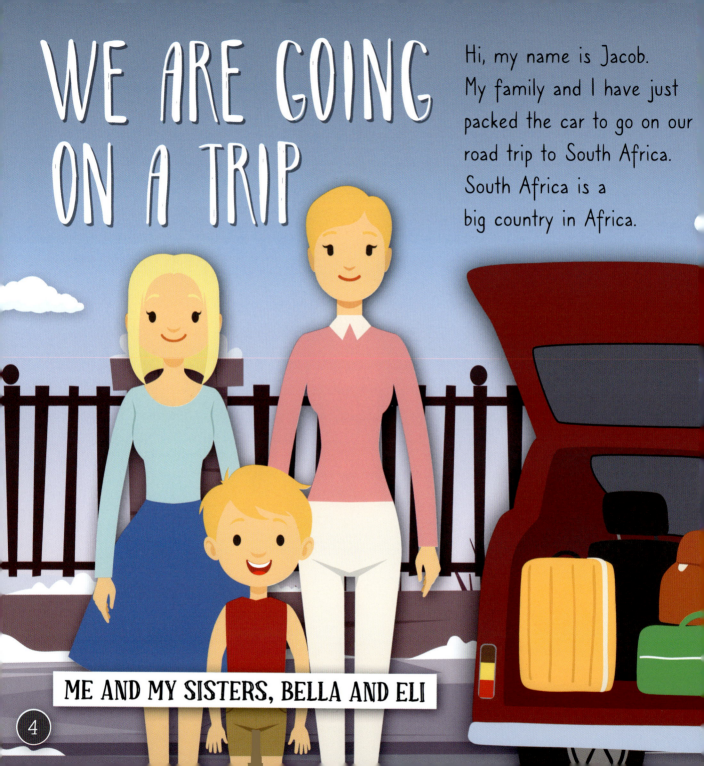

WE ARE GOING ON A TRIP

Hi, my name is Jacob. My family and I have just packed the car to go on our road trip to South Africa. South Africa is a big country in Africa.

ME AND MY SISTERS, BELLA AND ELI

Before we left, Eli gave me this map. It shows all the places that we will be going. I am going to follow the map to figure out where we will be going next!

KRUGER NATIONAL PARK

The first place we visit when we get to South Africa is Kruger National Park. We spot all of the animals in the African Big Five. The Big Five are: buffalo, elephants, leopards, lions, and rhinoceroses.

We see a baobab tree. It looks like it is upside down!

My favorite animal is the rhinoceros.

MOTLATSE CANYON

Motlatse <u>Canyon</u> is the third largest canyon in the world! It is covered in plants. We also see Bourke's Luck Potholes. The area was named after someone who tried to find gold there.

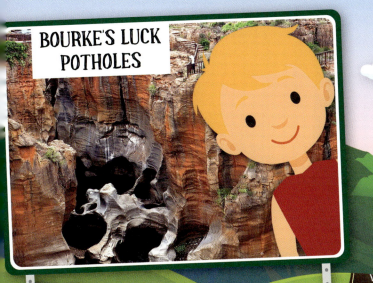

BOURKE'S LUCK POTHOLES

The view from above the canyon

This way: Motlatse Canyon

CRADLE OF HUMANKIND

I learn a lot of history at the Cradle of Humankind! There are lots of <u>fossils</u> and old tools, which show us how humans used to live and how we have changed over time.

THE CRADLE OF HUMANKIND

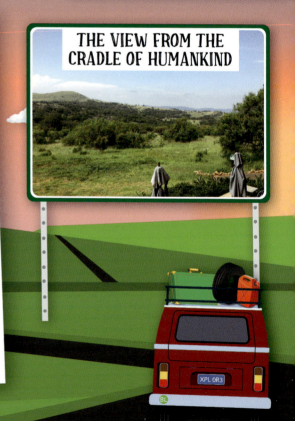

THE VIEW FROM THE CRADLE OF HUMANKIND

STERKFONTEIN CAVES

Some of the fossils at the Cradle of Humankind were found in the Sterkfontein <u>Caves</u>. We go on a tour of the caves. I learn all about how caves and fossils are formed.

INSIDE THE STERKFONTEIN CAVES

This was where some of the fossils were found!

JOHANNESBURG

Johannesburg is one of South Africa's largest cities. It is also known as the City of Gold! Even though it is a city, it has lots of nature. Johannesburg has around 10 million trees.

ISIMANGALISO WETLAND PARK

At iSimangaliso Wetland Park we see hippopotamuses, crocodiles, pelicans, and even flamingos. We find lots of the animals by St. Lucia Lake. The lake is connected to the sea, which makes it different than most lakes!

A HIPPOPOTAMUS IN THE LAKE

ST. LUCIA LAKE

Now entering: iSimangaliso Wetland Park

DRAKENSBERG

Some of the Drakensberg mountains are named after magical things! They are also known as the Dragon Mountains. Some of the highest mountains in South Africa are there. One of the mountains is called Giant's Castle.

We have a rest here before we start climbing!

GIANT'S CASTLE

Now entering: Drakensberg

THE BIG HOLE

The Big Hole used to be a diamond <u>mine</u>. This means that <u>precious</u> stones called diamonds were found here! We also go to the mining museum and learn how people got to the diamonds.

Now, the Big Hole is full of water.

Part of the mining museum was a mining village.

TSITSIKAMMA FOREST AND THE BIG TREE

We go for a walk in Tsitsikamma forest. We find a giant yellowwood tree. The tree is over 118 feet (36 m) tall. The distance around its <u>trunk</u> is about 29.5 feet (9 m)!

BATHURST

Bathurst is known for growing pineapples. Bathurst farmers tried to grow other things, but nothing other than pineapples would grow. To celebrate, they built a giant pineapple-shaped building and a pineapple museum.

THE BIG PINEAPPLE

PINEAPPLE FIELDS IN BATHURST

ADDO ELEPHANT NATIONAL PARK

To explore the elephant park, we go on a <u>safari</u>. At first, I do not think we will see many elephants. Then we get to the watering hole and there are lots of them!

An elephant joins us on the safari!

CAPE AGULHAS

Cape Agulhas is the farthest south it is possible to get in Africa. It also marks the place where two different oceans meet. We climb up a lighthouse to get a view of the ocean.

Now entering: Cape Agulhas

INDIAN OCEAN — ATLANTIC OCEAN

AFRIKAANS LANGUAGE MONUMENT

I learn about the history of the languages spoken in South Africa. One of the main languages is Afrikaans. We visit the Afrikaans Language Monument, which was built to celebrate how this language was made.

CAPE TOWN: V AND A WATERFRONT

The V and A Waterfront is South Africa's oldest working harbor. A harbor is a place near the sea where boats can <u>dock</u>. We go shopping at the market and try lots of new foods.

We ride on this big wheel!

TABLE MOUNTAIN

When I see it, I understand how Table Mountain got its name! Unlike many mountains that have a point on the top, Table Mountain is completely flat.

We get a cable car to the top of Table Mountain.

This way: Table Mountain

FALSE BAY

Our last stop is False Bay. Lots of sailors used to go to False Bay by mistake because they thought it was Table Bay. That is how it got its name!

We see penguins at Boulders Beach!

This way: False Bay

HOME

I had a great time in South Africa! From Kruger National Park to False Bay, there was so much to do. I loved seeing all the amazing animals. Seeing the Big Five was very exciting.

I cannot wait to go back to South Africa again! I would like to learn more about the country's history, maybe by visiting Robben Island.

Love, Jacob!

GLOSSARY

CANYON — a large valley with steep sides and a river flowing through it

CAVE — a large opening underground in rocks and hills

CELEBRATE — to do something special for an important event

DOCK — when a boat is brought in to land and tied up

FOSSIL — what is left of animals and plants from long ago that has been kept, or left its shape, in rock

MINE — underground tunnels that people have made to take out valuable things from the ground

PRECIOUS — very valuable

SAFARI — driving around to look at animals in their natural setting

TRUNK — the main woody stem of a tree

INDEX

animals 6, 11, 22

beaches 21

Big Five, the 6, 22

fossils 8–9

gold 7, 10

history 8, 18, 22

languages 18

lighthouses 17

mountains 12, 20

pineapples 15

trees 6, 10, 14